Design and Make
PUPPETS

Susie Hodge

W
FRANKLIN WATTS
LONDON·SYDNEY

Contents

Playing with puppets

This book is all about making puppets. It shows you how to design and make them with things you can find around your home. As well as puppets on a string, you can create simple puppets with a wooden spoon or even an old sock.

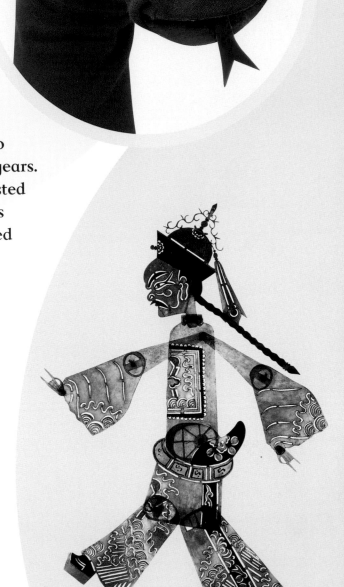

Telling a story

Puppets have been used by storytellers to explain and entertain for thousands of years. Puppet theatres are thought to have existed in most ancient civilisations. A puppet is a figure whose movements are controlled by someone using strings, rods or hand movements. Every generation reinvents puppets to suit their world and culture.

Playing with puppets

One of the oldest forms of puppet is believed to be the Chinese shadow puppet. Shadow puppets are cut-out figures, usually translucent and beautifully coloured. Puppets are placed close to a screen, and the light from a lamp placed behind them passes through the figures onto the screen. The audience, sitting on the other side of the screen, can see the colours and the outline of the puppets.

From flat to 3D

Rod puppets have also been used for thousands of years. These were beautifully carved and dressed according to the customs and myths of the country they were made in. Like shadow puppets, they were usually used to tell stories and to portray traditional characters. Many of these puppets have been uncovered in ancient Egyptian tombs and some had strings attached to them instead of rods.

Marionettes

Stringed puppets got their proper name, marionettes, in Europe during the third or fourth century AD. Puppeteers used to travel from town to town, performing the story of the Nativity on small stages built on the back of covered wagons. The stringed figure of the puppet portraying Mary was called a 'little Mary' or 'marionette', and the name stuck. Today, all puppets operated by strings are called marionettes.

Entertainment

Before the invention of radio and television, puppetry was a popular form of home entertainment. Many 18th- and 19th-century books contained instructions on how to make easy hand and string puppets. This book is a modern version with lots of ideas to design and make fun and simple puppets of your own.

Be prepared

Here is a list of all the materials and equipment you will need to make the different puppets in this book.

Hints and tips

* Always read the instructions all the way through BEFORE you start.
* Clear plenty of space to work in.
* Always check that you have everything you need and lay things out before you put your puppet together.
* Take time to think about your ideas. If you get stuck, talk your problem through with a friend or an adult.

Things to collect

PVA glue

Polystyrene and ping-pong balls

Balloons

Foam tennis ball

Paper fasteners

Plaster gauze

A selection of card, cardboard and paper (including tissue paper) in different sizes, colours and thicknesses

Plastic eyes

Odds and ends, such as cardboard tubes, old newspapers, feathers, silver foil, beads, bottle tops, yoghurt pots, ribbon, sequins, egg boxes, paper plates and cotton reels

Scraps of cloth, including felt, calico and other materials that won't fray easily

String, raffia and pipe cleaners

6

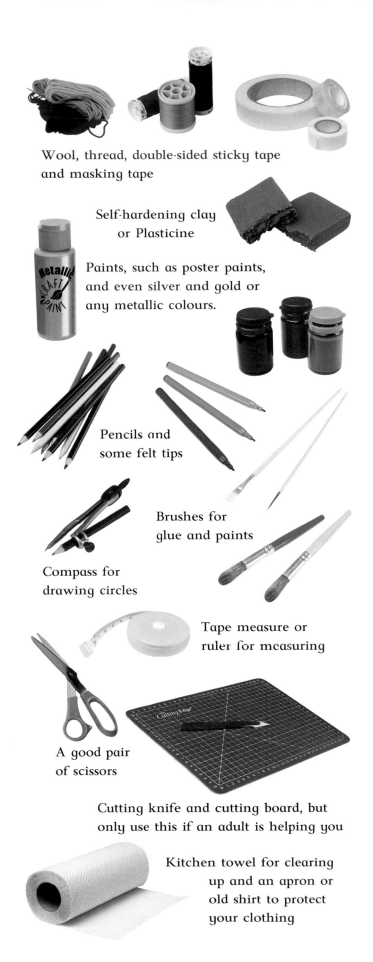

Wool, thread, double-sided sticky tape and masking tape

Self-hardening clay or Plasticine

Paints, such as poster paints, and even silver and gold or any metallic colours.

Pencils and some felt tips

Brushes for glue and paints

Compass for drawing circles

Tape measure or ruler for measuring

A good pair of scissors

Cutting knife and cutting board, but only use this if an adult is helping you

Kitchen towel for clearing up and an apron or old shirt to protect your clothing

Papier mâché

You will need:
an object (e.g. a balloon)
petroleum jelly
newspaper
brushes
PVA glue
(with a little water added)

Method
Smear some petroleum jelly over the object if you want to remove the papier mâché from it after it has dried. Tear the sheets of newspaper into small pieces or strips. Layer each piece of newspaper over the object, painting a fairly generous layer of diluted glue over each piece as you lay it down. Continue doing this until you have a good thickness. If you want a finer surface, use tissue paper for the top layers.

On your fingers

Finger puppets are fun to make and play with. You can make them out of card, paper or fabric, such as felt.

Design and select

Design your finger puppets with different faces, clothes and characters. Think about what you'll use for the body and details and draw a picture of your idea. Select your materials — we used some felt, wool, stick-on plastic eyes and felt-tip pens.

Look at this!

Finger puppets have amused babies, children and adults of all ages and nationalities for many years. These puppets are based on the fairytale Sleeping Beauty.

✱ How do you think they are decorated?

✱ How could you simplify the design?

Make

1 Based on your drawing, cut a strip of felt as long as your index or middle finger and about 6 cm wide, with two curved tops, as shown right.

2 Fold your felt in half so the curved tops line up and sew it together along the top and side seams. Don't sew up the bottom edge.

Challenge
Make finger puppets using card, where you use two of your fingers as the puppet's legs.

8

3 Once you have sewn all around the top and side of your puppet, turn it inside out. Cut a flesh-coloured circle out of felt for its face and glue this on.

Challenge
How could you make fabric, dangly legs for your finger puppet?

4 Cut a strip of felt to make the arms. Sew this onto the back of the body in the middle, be careful not to sew through both layers. Cut out some flesh-coloured felt hands and glue onto the end of each arm.

5 Using pieces of felt, make a nose, a collar, hat and bow tie, or whatever clothes you choose, and glue onto your puppet. Stick on the little plastic eyes, draw a smiley mouth with a red felt pen and stick wool or felt strips on the head for hair, and add a felt hat.

Challenge
Try making animal finger puppets, too.

Sock puppet

Make a simple but expressive puppet from a colourful sock.

Design and select

Design a snug hand puppet based on an old sock! Think about what kind of face or character your puppet will have. Will it be human or animal? What materials will you use to make it? Draw a picture of your idea and select your materials. We've chosen a sock, some plastic eyes, felt, card, paint and thread to make a dragon puppet.

Make

1 Try on your sock, placing the heel at the back of the wrist and putting your fingers and thumb in the toe. Try making it move! Make marks with a felt-tip pen where you will put the eyes, nose and mouth.

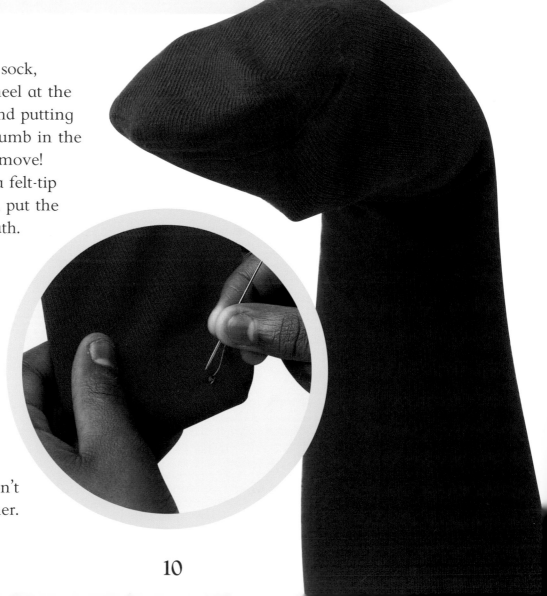

2 Make the nostrils by sewing over and over on the same spot. Before you do this, put a piece of card inside the sock so that you don't sew the sock together.

3 Stick on two plastic eyes above the nostrils.

4 To make the mouth, cut out a circle of card and score a line along the back across the centre to make it fold in half. Cut out a tongue with a forked end. Paint both pieces of card dark green.

Challenge
What other old item of clothing could you use to make a puppet?

5 Put your hand inside the puppet and glue on the mouth so that it fits between your fingers and thumb. Stick the tongue on top.

6 Cut out a strip of felt in the shape of spines and sew along the puppet's head.

Challenge
How could you give your puppet arms and legs?

7 Put your puppet on your hand and make it come alive!

Hand puppet

Make a hand puppet come alive by moving your fingers inside it.

Design and select

Design a hand puppet whose head and arms move. Think about what you will use to make it and sketch your idea. Select your materials — we've chosen felt, some marabou (feathery material), buttons, card, a balloon, paint and papier mâché for the head.

Make

1 Based on your drawing, create a card template for the puppet's body, with two arms and a neckline. Use your hand to work out its size.

2 Using the template, cut out two pieces of felt and sew them together. Leave a hole at the neck big enough for one of your fingers to poke through and leave the bottom edge open. Turn inside out so that the stitching doesn't show.

3 Blow up a balloon a little way and cover it with papier mâché (see page 7) to make the puppet's head. Build up the papier mâché in a small tube shape around the knot in the balloon to make the neck. It needs to be wide enough for your finger to poke through so that you can move the puppet's head.

4 When the papier mâché is drying, build up a little protruding nose and chin, using more, fairly soft papier mâché.

5 Leave the head to dry (this will take several hours) then burst the balloon with a sharp pencil. Paint the head in flesh colours. Paint on eyes and a mouth and stick on the marabou hair in a spiral shape, beginning in the centre of the back of the head and spiraling outwards.

Challenge
How could you adapt your puppet so it has legs as well?

6 Attach the head to the body by gluing the material around the neckline to the neck on the papier mâché head. Make hands out of felt and sew or glue them onto the arms. Add details, such as buttons and a felt collar. Slip on your hand puppet and create a character!

Spoon puppet

Use your imagination and make a puppet out of something that was never designed to be one!

Design and select

Design a wooden spoon puppet that can be animated by your finger and thumb. Think about what you will use for the body, whether you will add a hat or hair and draw a picture of your idea. Select your materials – we've used a wooden spoon, scraps of fabric, some thread, paint and wool.

Make

1 Draw a face carefully in pencil on the wooden spoon. Paint the face with flesh colours. Use a fine brush for the details like eyes and lips.

Challenge
How else could you make the spoon's face instead of painting it on?

2 Glue lengths of wool onto the top of the spoon to make hair. Plait these together on each side and tie the ends with wool. Glue on short pieces of wool to make a fringe.

3 To make a costume for your spoon puppet, cut out a circle of material. It needs to be big enough to cover your hand when you hold the spoon.

4 Cut a small hole in the centre of the material. Sew some thread around the edge of the hole using running stitch. Put the spoon through the hole, pull the thread to gather the material around the handle and tie a knot to hold it in place.

Challenge
What other household objects could you turn into a puppet?

5 Tape some bubble wrap or thick card around the neck of the spoon under the costume to help it stay in place. Wrap the last three fingers of your hand around the stick and use your forefinger and thumb as 'arms' and make your puppet move.

Jumping puppet

Create a puppet that comes alive with the pull of a string!

Design and select

Design a jumping-jack puppet whose arms and legs move. Think about what you will use for the body and how you will attach the limbs, allowing them to move at the same time. Draw a picture of your idea. Select your materials — we've chosen card, paints, paper fasteners, embroidery silk and a wooden bead.

Look at this!

This wooden jumping-jack puppet was made in Germany. Its legs and arms move when you tug the string.

✱ Which parts of the body do you think are attached to each other?

✱ What other parts of the puppet could be made to move as well?

Make

1 Cut out the head and body shape of your puppet out of card, and the leg and arm shapes. They need to be similar to the shapes we have cut out (right), but they can vary according to your design.

Head

Arm

Body

Arm

Leg

Leg

2 Pierce a hole with a needle at the top of the head and at the shoulder on the arm and leg parts.

Challenge
What other materials could you use to make the body, legs and arms?

16

3 On the head and body part, draw on the face, clothes and other details with a pencil. Cut out some coloured card shapes for the other clothes and stick onto your figure. Paint on details for the face, hair and hands.

4 To attach the arm and leg parts, push a paper fastener through either side of the body near the shoulders (see left) and through each leg and arm piece (see below), one on either side. Open out the fasteners on the back.

5 Thread some embroidery silk through the hole in the head, make a loop and tie a knot in the end. Thread another piece of embroidery silk through the holes in both arms, add a colourful bead and then knot the ends together, as shown above.

Challenge
How could you make another part of the body move?

6 Hold the puppet by the top loop and tug on your bead to make your puppet dance!

Looking at faces

Make your puppets come alive
with different expressions and faces!

Look at this!

In most popular stories, there are good and
bad characters. Punch and Judy are a traditional
seaside puppet show. This puppet (right) is
a traditional Punch and Judy character and
always had a scary personality.

✱ How have this puppet's features been
exaggerated to make it more scary?

Design and select

Practise creating different faces for puppets using different materials.
Look at some puppets with strong facial expressions or characteristics,
such as Pinocchio or Punch and Judy. Design different puppet faces
that will bring your puppets' characters alive and select your
materials. We've used a balloon, papier mâché, wadding, felt,
a Styrofoam ball, old tights, craft hair and paint.

Make

1 Partly blow up a balloon. Cover it in papier mâché
(see page 7). Make sure that there aren't any
gaps and then begin to build up the nose with more
papier mâché, layering it to form a triangular shape.

2 When the papier mâché is dry, you can paint the head.
Give your head whatever personality you choose!
This head is quite angular, which can seem quite scary.
We have given it bloodshot eyes for extra effect!

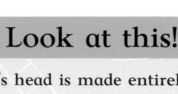

Look at this!

This puppet's head is made entirely from felt.

✱ How does the felt head help to soften the puppet's features?

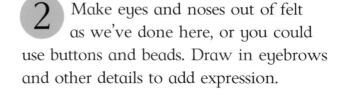

1 Make simple faces for your puppets by cutting out circles of felt for head shapes. Stick on different coloured pieces of felt for the features.

2 Make eyes and noses out of felt as we've done here, or you could use buttons and beads. Draw in eyebrows and other details to add expression.

3 You can either just stick the faces on your puppet as they are, or you could sew another piece of felt to the back and stuff them with wadding to make them head-shaped.

Look at this!

This queen marionette has a very jolly, happy face.

✱ What would you need to change to make her look angry?

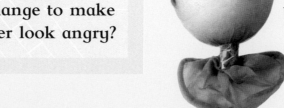

1 Roll a tiny piece of wadding or cotton wool into a ball and stick it onto a Styrofoam ball. The wadding becomes the nose! Cover the ball with the toe cut from a pair of old tights. Tape this together tightly at the bottom to make the neck.

2 Glue on some hair and two plastic eyes or buttons. Stitch or paint on a mouth. This face could be Grandma's from Red Riding Hood!

Expressive head

Create a lively puppet head that could be used for a marionette or hand puppet.

Look at this!

This puppet was handmade for a play. The features have been exaggerated to look expressive.

✱ What kind of character do you think this puppet has?

Design and select

Design a puppet head that shows a strong character. Like a caricature, you need to make just one or two features particularly striking. Think about what personality you want to portray. What materials will you use? Draw a picture of your idea, and then select your materials. We've made a sinister character using a foam tennis ball, plaster gauze, a pencil, paint, craft hair and felt.

Make

1 Cover your work surface with old newspapers and protect your clothes with an apron or old shirt. Use plaster gauze to cover a foam tennis ball. It is important that you do not get the plaster in your eyes, so always wash your hands after using it and don't rub your eyes while working.

2 Cut the plaster gauze into small strips. Dip each strip into a bowl of water and squeeze down gently, spreading the plaster across the holes of the gauze. Layer the strips around the ball until you have covered it completely.

3 Continue to layer the plaster gauze over the ball, gradually building up the chin, forehead, nose, eyes and eyebrows. Exaggerate the type of character you are making.

Challenge
What other materials could you use to make the eyes?

4 Push a pencil or stick into the base of the head and build up the plaster around the pencil to make the neck. Leave the head to dry, then, holding the pencil, paint the face, concentrating on your puppet's character.

5 Using wool, craft hair or shredded crêpe paper, make a wig for your head! Stick the wig to your puppet. Make a simple hat out of felt.

Challenge
How does the hair give the head a different character? What could you use to alter the puppet's personality by changing its hair?

Challenge
Make hands and feet for your puppet using the same plaster gauze method. What could you use to make the body of your puppet?

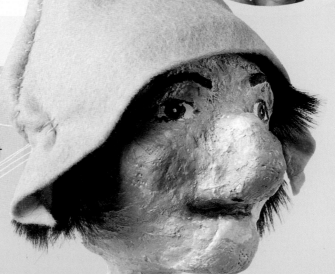

21

Lucy long limbs

Make a puppet that sits still, but you can move his or her arms with attached sticks.

Look at this!

The Wayang Goleck puppets from Java are mounted on a finely carved stick that forms the body, and supports and turns the head. The arms are held up and moved by two long sticks made of wood, bone or ivory.

✳ How do you think the arms bend?

✳ What other parts of the body could you make move using rods?

Design and select

Design a puppet whose body is firm, but whose arms move. Draw a picture of your idea and think about what materials you will use. Select your materials. We've used a sock, a plastic bag, a Styrofoam ball, pair of tights, some fabric, wadding, sand, paints, card, wool, tassels, ribbon and pipe cleaners.

Make

1 Based on your drawing, fill a plastic bag with sand and then place inside an old sock to make a body. Tie a knot in the sock to make the neck.

2 Wrap a piece of fabric around the body and sew it together at the back and bottom (leave the top open to attach the head later).

3 Make a head using a Styrofoam ball, with a piece of wadding for the nose and covered in the toe of a pair of tights (see page 19). Paint on the features. To make the hair, gather together some brown wool to fit across the head. Use tassels and ribbon to make bunches.

4 Make two long sleeves out of the same fabric that covers the body. Cut two long pieces of the fabric, fold them in half lengthways with the right-sides together. Sew up along the long edges and then turn them the right way out. Make two hands out of card and staple to the end of each arm. Sew the arms onto the body at the shoulders.

5 Make trousers in the same way as you made the arms, sew these on to the underside of your puppet's body and staple some card shoe shapes at the end.

6 Twist two pipe cleaners together and staple these to the card hands to make the arms move. Prop your puppet up on a table or box and make it come to life!

Challenge
How could you make the legs move as well as the arms?

Shadow puppets

Shadow puppets have been used for centuries, all over the world. You can make illusions and clever effects by shining a light behind the puppets to create a shadow on a screen.

Look at this!

This is an antique Chinese shadow puppet made of animal hide.

✱ How do you think this puppet is moved?

✱ What sort of character do you think this puppet would have in a story?

Design and select

Design a shadow puppet with moving limbs. Think about how you will project the shadows onto a screen. What sort of light will you use? How will you create a white screen? Design the shadow puppets you would like and select your materials. We've used black card, a straw and paper fasteners.

Make

1 Based on your design, draw the outline shapes of your shadow puppet on some paper. The limbs need to be separate from the body so that you can cut them out.

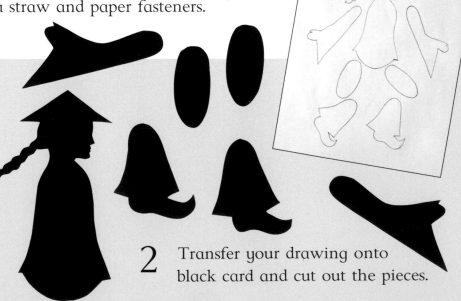

2 Transfer your drawing onto black card and cut out the pieces.

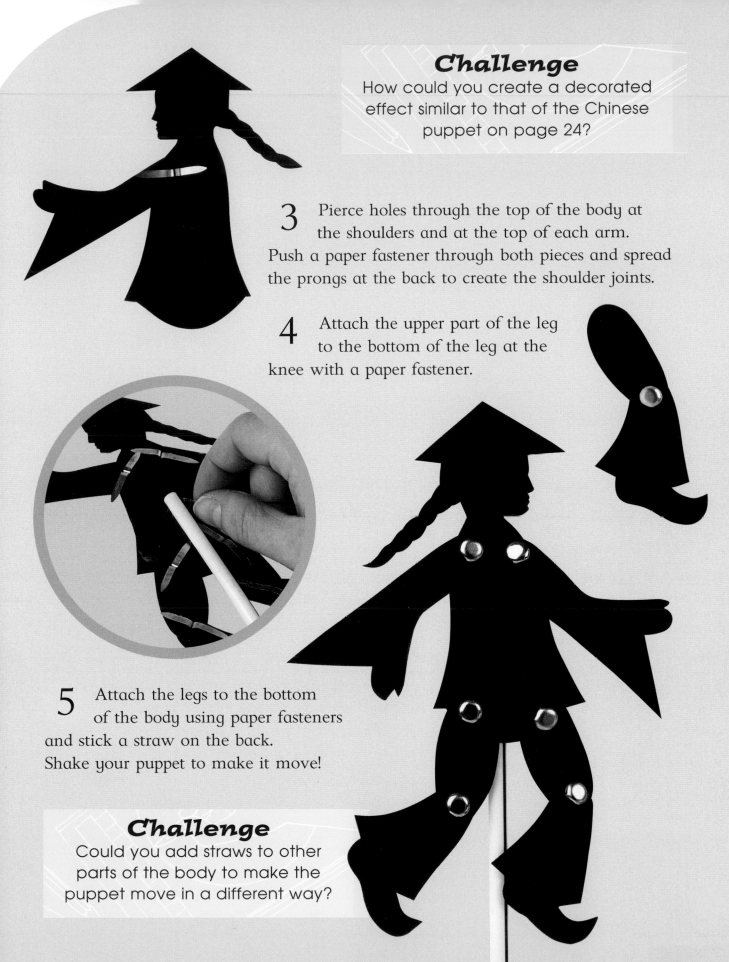

Challenge

How could you create a decorated effect similar to that of the Chinese puppet on page 24?

3   Pierce holes through the top of the body at the shoulders and at the top of each arm. Push a paper fastener through both pieces and spread the prongs at the back to create the shoulder joints.

4   Attach the upper part of the leg to the bottom of the leg at the knee with a paper fastener.

5   Attach the legs to the bottom of the body using paper fasteners and stick a straw on the back. Shake your puppet to make it move!

Challenge

Could you add straws to other parts of the body to make the puppet move in a different way?

On a string

A puppet on a string – or a marionette – is a favourite in puppet theatres. The strings enable the puppets to be moved in all sorts of dramatic ways.

Design and select

Think about the puppet you would like to make. What kind of hair will it have? What kind of clothes will it wear? Sketch out your idea. Select your materials – we used lolly sticks, cardboard, scraps of fabric, thread, a ping-pong ball, wool, paint, sequins and Plasticine.

Look at this!

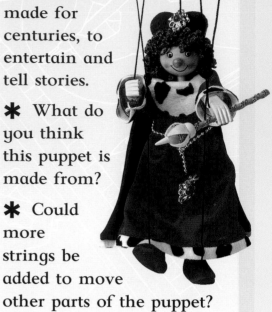

Marionettes have been made for centuries, to entertain and tell stories.

✱ What do you think this puppet is made from?

✱ Could more strings be added to move other parts of the puppet?

Make

1 Following your picture, make a head out of a ping-pong ball and a wooden lolly stick. Pierce a hole in the ping-pong ball with sharp scissors and push the stick into it. This will be the head and neck.

2 Scrunch up a small piece of tissue paper and glue it on the ping-pong ball to make the nose. Paint on a face and glue on hair made from short strands of wool tied together. We've made a prince so have finished off the head with a felt and sequin crown.

Challenge
What else could you use to make the head?

3 Roll up a piece of cardboard for the body and glue it together. The lolly stick will slot into this when you attach the head.

4 Make hands out of Plasticine to give weight to your puppet. Push half a lolly stick into each hand.

Challenge
How could you make the legs have joints in them?

5 Use felt to make a shirt for your puppet. Cut out a cross shape, as shown right, with a hole for the neck. Stick on the hands and sew up or glue the edges, but leave holes for the neck and arms, and at the bottom.

6 Use scrap fabric to make the trousers. Cut out two trouser shapes and sew together at the sides and between the legs. Make feet in the same way you made the hands and glue the legs inside the trousers so the feet stick out of the ends. Put the trousers and top onto the cardboard body you made earlier. Then stick on the head.

7 Glue two lolly sticks together to make the cross bar. Tie thread round the four ends of the sticks and one in the centre. Attach the central string to the top of the head, the front strings to the arms and the back strings to the legs. The strings need to be long enough so that the legs and arms can hang down properly. Now make your puppet dance!

A puppet theatre

You can make puppets move on their own, but why not make a puppet theatre and put on a puppet play! You can make a theatre out of almost anything. For instance, you could drape a large sheet or blanket over the back of a sofa or two chairs and hide behind this, working your puppets from there.

Finger puppet theatres

This theatre works well with finger puppets, glove or hand puppets. Find a large box and cut out a window in the side (ask an adult to help you with this). Paint or cover the box in paper, fabric or sticky-back plastic. Open out the bottom flaps and cut off the back one. Place the box on the edge of a table and work the puppets by placing your hands up through the opening. Make curtains out of scrap pieces of material and staple these onto your theatre.

Marionette theatres

A marionette theatre needs to have a hole in the top so that you can dangle the puppets down onto the stage. Find a large cardboard box and cut a hole in the front and top. You can make curtains for this or simply drape some fabric or a towel over the front.

Shadow puppet theatre

A shadow puppet theatre needs a hole in the front and back of a cardboard box. Cut out a rectangle from a thin, white plastic bag and stretch it across the hole in the front of the box. Stick the plastic down securely with tape. Keep the screen taut – if it sags or wrinkles, it will spoil the performance. Put the box on its side on the edge of a table. Shine a lamp or torch behind the screen. Put your shadow puppet between the screen and the light source and begin your shadow show.

Developing a play

Once you have made a theatre you need to decide what sort of show your puppets are going to perform. You can make up your own play or choose a story that you know. Practise moving your puppet – exaggerate its movements. Keep the puppet facing the audience as much as possible and remember that with puppets, action works better than words. Move your puppet in character before it appears and don't let it simply pop on to the stage as this will destroy the illusion.

Scenery and sound

Simple scenery is often the most effective. You can use a plain backdrop of light blue cloth, for instance, or paint scenes and fix them to the back of your stage with tape. Any props need to be simple and just suggestive of an idea, rather than something elaborate. Music will set the mood for your play, but don't make it too loud. Use musical instruments or a tape or CD player.

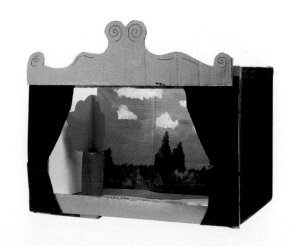

Glossary

ancestors
members of your family who lived long before you

animated
something that is made to look alive

caricature
a picture or description of a person or thing that exaggerates their features or personality

characteristics
features, type or description

diluted
watered down

elaborate
intricate or ornate, over-complicated

extend
lengthen or make longer

flexible
able to bend

Java
the largest island of Indonesia

marabou
a soft, fluffy strip of material, available in various colours

protruding
sticking out

right side
the side of the material you want to show

taut
stretched tight

template
outline, pattern or guide

transfer
move on to another surface

translucent
slightly see-through

wadding
padding usually used for stuffing soft toys

Further information

You might find these websites helpful for finding ideas and techniques:

www.ppo.co.uk
To see lots of pictures of the traditional Pelham puppets.

www.ex.ac.uk/bill.douglas/ schools/shadows/shadows1.htm
Information about shadow puppets with lots of good pictures. Instructions for making hand shadows, too.

http://discover-indo.tierranet.com /wayang.html
Lots of information and pictures of shadow puppets.

www.mandalaymarionettes.com
Website about Myanmar puppet theatre with pictures showing how the puppets are made and decorated.

www.puppetplanet.co.uk
Puppet shop with many antique and new puppets including Thunderbirds, Pelham and also traditional African, Indian and Burmese puppets.

www.puppetryindia.org
Website featuring lots of pictures of different types of Indian puppets and information about them.

http://www.sagecraft.com/ puppetry/traditions/
Website with links to other sites about many different puppets all over the world.

http://welcome.to/karagoz
Lots of information and pictures of Turkey's traditional shadow puppet play, Karagoz.

http://www.vietscape.com/travel /hanoi/puppet.html
Webpage about Vietnamese water puppets.

http://www.balibeyond.com/ cswayang.html
Links to videos of Balinese shadow puppets plays.

Index

First published in 2005 by
Franklin Watts, 96 Leonard Street
London EC2A 4XD

Franklin Watts Australia
Level 17/207 Kent Street, Sydney, NSW 2000

© Franklin Watts 2005

Editor: Rachel Tonkin; Art Director: Jonathan Hair;
Design: Matthew Lilly and Anna-Marie D'Cruz;
Photography: Steve Shott.

The publisher wishes to thank Lesley Butler, Puppet Planet,
Wandsworth, London for the loan of the puppets on pp 4, 5, 12,
16, 18, 19, 20, 22 and 24.

A CIP catalogue record for this book
is available from the British Library

Dewey Classification: 745.592'2

ISBN 0 7496 6072 4

Printed in China